GEO

8/16
Lexile: _____

AR/BL: _____

AR Points: _____

Myths of
OCEANIA

Anita Dalal

RAINTREE
STECK-VAUGHN
PUBLISHERS

A Harcourt Company

Austin   New York
www.raintreesteckvaughn.com

Steck-Vaughn Company

First published 2002 by Raintree Steck-Vaughn Publishers, an imprint of Steck-Vaughn Company.

Library of Congress Cataloging-in-Publication Data

Dalal, Anita.
     Myths of Oceania / Anita Dalal.
         p. cm. -- (Mythic world)
     Includes bibliographical references and index.
     ISBN 0-7398-4978-6

Printed and bound in the United States
1 2 3 4 5 6 7 8 9 0 IP 05 04 03 02 01

Series Consultant: C. Scott Littleton, Professor of Anthropology,
Occidental College, Los Angeles
Volume Author: Anita Dalal

for Brown Partworks Limited
Project Editor: Lee Stacy
Designer: Sarah Williams
Picture Researcher: Helen Simm
Cartographer: Mark Walker
Indexer: Kay Ollerenshaw
Managing Editor: Tim Cooke
Design Manager: Lynne Ross
Production Manager: Matt Weyland

for Raintree Steck-Vaughn
Project Editor: Sean Dolan
Production Manager: Richard Johnson

Contents

General Introduction

MYTHS ARE THE MIRRORS of humanity. They reflect the inner soul of a culture and try to give profound answers in a seemingly mysterious world. In other words, myths give the relevant culture an understanding of its place in the world and the universe in general. Found in all civilizations, myths sometimes combine fact and fiction and other times are complete fantasy. Regardless of their creative origin, myths are always dramatic.

Every culture has its own myths, yet globally there are common themes and symbols, even across civilizations that had no contact with or awareness of each other. Some of the most common types include those that deal with the creation of the world, the cosmos, or a particular site, like a large mountain or lake. Other myths deal with the origin of humans, or a specific people or civilization, or the heroes or gods who either made the world inhabitable or gave humans something essential, such as the ancient Greek Titan Prometheus, who gave fire, or the Ojibwa hero Wunzh, who was given divine instructions on cultivating corn. There are also myths about the end of the world, death and the afterlife, and the renewal or change of seasons.

The origin of evil and death are also common themes. Examples of such myths are the Biblical Eve eating the forbidden fruit or the ancient Greek story of Pandora opening the sealed box.

Additionally there are flood myths, myths about the sun and the moon, and myths of a peaceful, beautiful place of reward, such as heaven or Elysium, or of punishment, such as hell or Tartarus. Myths also teach important human values, such as courage. In all cases, myths show that the gods and their deeds are outside of ordinary human life and yet essential to it.

In this volume some of the most important myths of the vast Pacific area known as Oceania are presented. Following each myth is an explanation of how the myth was either reflected in or linked to the real life of the different peoples of Oceania. There is also a glossary at the end of the volume to help identify the major mythological and historical characters as well as explain many cultural terms.

MYTHOLOGY OF OCEANIA

Oceania is a massive area of the Pacific Ocean that covers over 3 million square miles (8.5 million sq. km). It stretches from Australia and New Zealand in the extreme southwest to Hawaii in the north and Easter Island in the east. Lying within this enormous region are thousands of islands that, in addition to Australia, comprise three distinct culture areas, Melanesia, Micronesia, and Polynesia.

Yet in spite of the thousands of miles between the islands there are strong similarities among

Above: *Oceania covers a large part of the Pacific Ocean and includes thousands of islands, large and small. In addition to Australia, the major geographical regions are Micronesia, Melanesia, and the largest, Polynesia.*

the myths of Melanesia, Micronesia, and Polynesia. The Australian Aborigines, however, have their own unique belief system unrelated to the rest of Oceania.

Aboriginal mythology is based on the idea of "Dreamtime." Dreamtime was an age when humans and the natural world were created. Many Aborigines believe that Dreamtime continues and it is where ancestral spirits live.

Unlike the outback setting of the Aboriginal myths, many of the myths in the rest of Oceania are about the sea, fishing, and other aspects of island living. There are also myths and deities unique to individual island cultures. For example, Hawaii, which has the world's highest level of volcanic activity, has myths about Pele, goddess of volcanoes, and rituals are performed year-round to appease the angry goddess.

Black-headed Python the Widow

The Worora Aborigines began the story of Black-headed Python's sad journey across Australia, a journey that witnessed the creation of many plants and animals.

URING THE AGE OF Dreamtime, Native Cat and his wife, Black-headed Python, had a very happy life together until one day Native Cat got sick. His body became completely covered in sores and Black-headed Python tried everything she could think of to cure him. Nothing worked. Eventually Native Cat died. After burying her husband Black-headed Python set off, alone, toward the east.

She traveled for a long time until she came to a place where a goanna lizard was buried. Black-headed Python poked the grave and gave it the name of Marngut. Having named the place, she carried on with her journey until she arrived at a small hill called Wunjaragin, also known as Loose Mountain.

The hill seemed to be crumbling. Black-headed Python stooped down and gathered up some of the mud from the hill. Then she tried to bind it together using strands of her hair, but the mud would not stay in one piece. It kept breaking apart. After she had spent much time trying to save the hill, some bull ants appeared and helped her bind the mud together. Once the hill was rebuilt, Black-headed Python set off again.

As she traveled across the land she paused at various points and marked the ground. At each place she created different plants and animals. But Black-headed Python did not stop to nurture her creations; instead the lonely widow continued her solitary journey.

In the meantime Blue-tongued Lizard had visited the grave of Native Cat. He had heard Black-headed Python crying when she buried her husband, and Blue-tongued Lizard did not like to see his friend unhappy. So Blue-tongued Lizard brought Native Cat back to life.

Together, Blue-tongued Lizard and Native Cat set off to find Black-headed Python. But when she eventually saw her husband, Black-headed Python was angry. She cried out, "Go back to your grave! I am a widow now. I have cut off all my hair and am bald. And I have covered my face with charcoal dust so that everyone I meet knows I am a widow. Go back to your grave, reenter it, and die."

Native Cat could see that his wife meant what she said, so he obeyed her. Ever since that time, many widows have followed the example of Black-headed Python and cut off their hair and rubbed their faces with charcoal.

Above: *Australian Aborigines painted representations of their mythological characters, such as Black-headed Python and Blue-tongued Lizard, on rocks, cliff-faces, and, as shown here, on dried bark.*

Origins and Lifestyles of Australian Aborigines

For 40,000 years the Australian Aborigines have survived in a hostile environment. Their beliefs provide an explanation for the harsh world around them and their own existence.

The story of Black-headed Python (see page 6) is a type of creation myth from the Worora people of northwestern Australia and illustrates two very important aspects of Australian Aboriginal beliefs. First, every Aboriginal group, or tribe, has its own version of how things came to be during the period of creation of their ancestors, known as "Dreamtime" (also called "Alchera"). Second, the myth explains how a group's beliefs and habits began.

FIRST ABORIGINES

It is thought that the earliest ancestors of the Aborigines arrived in Australia some 40,000 years ago. Because of its distant position in the Pacific Ocean, Australia, the world's smallest continent, was not charted by Europeans until the British explorer Captain James Cook (1728–1779) landed there in the 18th century — although archaeologists now know the Aborigines had

Left: *This 1891 illustration is based on a photograph of an Aborigine mother and her child outside their hut. In the 19th century, as British settlers explored Australia, some documented the daily lives of its native inhabitants, the Aborigines.*

experienced some extended contact with people from New Guinea and Indonesia long before.

By the time of Cook's arrival, the Aborigines had been leading a semi-nomadic lifestyle for thousands of years. Those on the Australian coast were skilled fishermen, and the groups who lived in the interior or outback hunted animals and birds as their main food source.

The Aborigines were extremely knowledgeable about and sensitive to every aspect of the land they inhabited, including climate, sources of water, and plant life. Aboriginal groups were made up of extended families. Those who lived in the interior inhabited areas close to fresh water not only for survival but because they believed the spirits of their ancestors dwelled there. Even today traditional Aborigines prefer to live on ancestral land and rarely consider moving to new areas.

WORSHIPING NATURE

The Aborigines also view all of nature as being sacred because all of nature was created by spirits of the Dream-time. For example, the winding Ord and Victoria rivers are believed to have

been formed by Black-headed Python because they resemble the meandering shape of a snake.

The Aborigines also worshiped particular animals. These became tribal symbols, known anthropologically as totems. Each tribe had its own symbol, including unique Australian animals such as wallabies and dingoes.

Above: *Archae-ologists believe that the grooves in these stones were made by ancient Aborigines for ax grinding.*

Unique Wildlife

Because it is so isolated from Southeast Asia and the rest of the world, Australia has many species of animals native only to the island continent. Examples include the koala, the kangaroo, and the duck-billed platypus. In the Aborigine belief system human beings were once other types of animals and plants. They believe that all the natural beings on earth, including human beings, are interchangeable. Also, particular places on the earth are thought to be uniquely associated with a particular animal.

Above: *Koalas and other marsupials, such as kangaroos, are unique to Australia.*

Rainbow Snake and Tjinimin

This creation myth originated with the Murinbata Aborigines of the Northern Territory. Out of Rainbow Snake's wound came all-important water supplies for the dry outback.

O<small>NE DAY</small> T<small>JINIMIN</small> the Bat pretended he was going to visit his relatives, the flying fox people. Instead, he secretly followed his sisters, the green parrot women, as they left the village in search of food. Once they were far away from the village, Tjinimin snuck up on his sisters and attacked them. After they recovered, the green parrot women vowed to take revenge on their brother.

The green parrot women carried on searching for food, and Tjinimin, who wanted to attack them again, continued stalking them. This time the sisters were ready for Tjinimin. When they crossed an estuary ahead of him they summoned a swarm of hornets to sting him all over his body. Tjinimin jumped in the water to escape the hornets, but his sisters made the tide carry him far out to sea.

Eventually Tjinimin managed to swim back to shore. He spied the green parrot women's fire on top of a cliff and called out to them for help. They agreed to throw down a rope and pull him up. The sisters waited until he had almost reached the top before cutting the rope. Tjinimin crashed to the rocks below, breaking all his bones. At first he

thought he would die. Then Tjinimin wished that his body would heal. He wished very hard, and in an instant his broken bones mended. Tjinimin had discovered that he possessed magic powers.

Realizing the strength of his powers, Tjinimin next plotted to kill his father, Rainbow Snake (also known as Kunmanggur). He returned to the village, bringing with him a spear that he pretended belonged to Rainbow Snake. Tjinimin invited everyone to a big ceremony where his father played the drone pipe while Tjinimin led the dancing. During one dance, he drew out the spear and stabbed his father. Immediately all the dancers turned into flying foxes and birds and flew off, crying with grief. Tjinimin fled, too.

Rainbow Snake went from place to place as he tried to find a way to stop the blood pouring from his wound. Wherever he stopped life-giving water gushed out of the ground. This water allowed plants and people to live in the dry landscape. As Rainbow Snake slithered on, in one place he left the shape of his body and his footprints on a rock wall. In other places he left his possessions, including his stone ax, fishing net, and forehead band.

Above: *In the harsh, dry conditions of the outback, springs and watering holes are essential for survival. Aborigines honored Rainbow Snake for providing sources of water.*

Rainbow Snake continued his journey until, at last, he came to the sea. As he entered the sea, he gathered all the fire of the world and put it on his head as a kind of headdress. His distraught followers watched him as he stepped into the water and they suddenly realized that their great leader was not going to stop. He would take the fire of the world with him. They tried to snatch the last flame, but they were not able to reach it in time. Later, the hero spirit Pilirin the Kestrel gave back fire to humans by rubbing two sticks together to create sparks.

Aborigine Dreamtime

For non-Aborigines, it is difficult to understand the concept of Dreamtime. It is both an ancient age when spirits roamed the earth and also an age that exists now as another dimension where spirits and ancestors still dwell.

Left: *An Aborigine musician plays a didgeridoo, a traditional wind instrument. The setting is an ancient Aborigine sacred place (note the handprints and painted kangaroo on the rocks).*

In Aborigine mythology, Rainbow Snake is one of the most important figures. In "Rainbow Snake and Tjinimin" (see page 10), he is responsible for creating life even though he is mortally wounded. Rainbow Snake belongs both to the landscape and to Dreamtime, the era of creation when ancestral spirits walked the earth — although for many peoples, Dreamtime is ongoing. All Aborigines believe that during Dreamtime spirits rose up from the ground and roamed the earth.

During Dreamtime the ancestors took on the shapes of animals and plants and traveled across Australia. As they traveled, they created the world: They gave rivers their meandering paths, they created Uluru — known also as Ayer's Rock — they made people and left behind the spirits of all those who still had to be born. A basic Aborigine belief is that all of life — past and present — is interconnected and exists in one vast network. This interconnectedness is reflected in the landscape itself, which is why all Aborigines worship the land.

An Aborigine tribe consisted of several local groups or bands. They stayed together for most of the year, if they had a sufficient food supply. Tribes would always settle where their ancestors had originally lived and where they believed the spirits of the clan continued to exist while they waited to be reincarnated. Each people's territory centered on a watering hole. If some tribe members had to leave to find a new water source, they would remain the kinsfolk of the original tribe.

Each tribe's myths describe the different wanderings of their clan's ancestral hero. For example, Rainbow Snake's journey is reenacted by the Murinbata people. To contact the spirits of the Dreamtime, a tribe's chief enters a state of consciousness similar to dreaming. In that dreamlike state it is believed the chief can receive revelations and instructions from the ancestors. All Aboriginal myths, songs, and ceremonies are received in this state.

SACRED ULURU

Central to all Aboriginal peoples was keeping their ancestors' spirits alive by chanting. The spirits were present in every aspect of the landscape and daily life. All the tribes have sacred places where the spirits of the ancestors are felt strongly. One of the most sacred places is Uluru — or Ayer's Rock — almost in the

Above: *Uluru, a sacred Aborigine site rising out of the brushland, is also known as Ayer's Rock.*

Below: *A sacred Dreamtime disc representing an immortal spirit.*

exact geographical center of Australia. Its name means "meeting place." Around the base of the giant red rock are Aboriginal paintings, thousands of years old, that describe different creation myths of Dreamtime.

Another important aspect of Dreamtime are the "Footprints of the Ancestors," also known as "Dreaming tracks" or "songlines." Aborigines believe that the whole of the Australian continent is connected by an ancient series of invisible tracks and that these tracks are made of songs that tell of the Dreamtime and the period of creation. It is vital to every Aborigine that the songs are passed on from generation to generation. One of their most important sacred duties is to travel across the land following the songline of their particular totem — such as the Rainbow Snake — and sing the songs of their ancestors. By doing this, they are reconfirming the creation and linking the past to the present.

Separation of the Earth and Sky

This Maori myth from New Zealand is known across Polynesia and has strong similarities to myths from faraway cultures, such as the Egyptian myth of Nut (the sky) and Geb (the earth).

BEFORE THE BEGINNING of time the only things that existed were the sun, the two gods, Rangi and Papa, and their six sons. Rangi was the god of the sky and Papa was the earth goddess, and they loved each other so much that they were locked in a passionate, permanent embrace. But the parent-gods' embrace was so tight that not even sunlight could pass between them. Without sunlight, Papa the earth was shrouded in darkness.

One day, the sons of Rangi and Papa held a meeting. Each of them was the god of something on earth or in the sky, but they all had different strengths and characters. The sons decided that they had to stop their parents' embracing in order to admit the sunlight.

At first the brothers struggled to agree on a solution. Tu-matauenga, the god of war and the most aggressive of the sons, suggested that they should kill their parents. But Tane-mahuta, the god of forests and everything in them, refused. Instead, he argued that the brothers should separate their parents so that their father would rise up high into the heavens, well out of reach of their mother's tight embrace.

The other brothers agreed with Tane-mahuta, all except Tawhiri-matea, the god of winds and storms, who did not want sunlight because he was worried that too much of it might destroy the bad weather that he wanted to create. So Tawhiri-matea sat back and did nothing as each brother tried in vain to separate their parents.

Rongo-ma-Tane, the god of cultivated food, was the first to try to separate his parents, but he failed. Then, Tangaroa, the god of all things living in the sea, and Haumia-tiketike, the god of uncultivated food, each took their own turn at trying to break their parents' embrace. But they too failed.

Then the fierce Tu-matauenga created a machete and used it to hack at Rangi, causing him to bleed. This turned the sky a blood-red color that can still be seen today at every sunset. Despite Rangi's wound the couple continued to cling to each other.

Finally it was Tane-mahuta's turn to separate Rangi and Papa. First he used his arms to try to pry his parents apart, but he failed. Then, after a long pause, he put his shoulders against his mother and his feet against his father and began pushing.

Above: *This Maori wood carving of Rangi and Papa shows the embracing couple surrounded by their sons. The faces of the gods are darkly decorated. Maori warriors tattooed their own faces in much the same way.*

Very slowly the two parent-gods started to come apart. The sinews attaching the earth to the sky stretched and ripped. Both Rangi and Papa let out loud howls of pain and misery as they gradually got pushed farther and farther away from each other. Tane-mahuta continued to use all his strength, which was the same strength that made the trees grow. He pushed and pushed until his parents were too far apart to touch each other. Rangi cried and his tears were the only part of him that could reach Papa: They still fall as the rain from the sky. Papa was inconsolable with grief, and to this day her sighs of longing still rise up to the sky as the mists that cover the earth.

Migrating Across the Pacific Ocean

The journeys of the Polynesian peoples across the Pacific Ocean in their canoes is one of humankind's most adventurous and courageous achievements.

The story of separating Rangi from Papa (see page 14) originated with the Maori, a Polynesian people who settled in New Zealand. Polynesia is the name given to the islands in the central and southern Pacific, including Hawaii, Easter Island, and New Zealand. Another important island group is Melanesia, northwest of Australia (see map on page 5), which was the cradle of the many different Polynesian cultures.

About 3000 B.C. in Melanesia, which includes New Guinea, the Solomon Islands, and Fiji, peoples from Southeast Asia encountered peoples who spoke languages called Austronesian. Over the centuries the groups interbred, creating different peoples who migrated eastward throughout Polynesia.

Early Polynesians were motivated to travel to new islands for various reasons, including trade, the need for new resources, colonization, war,

overcrowding, and simple curiosity. The first islands settled by Polynesians were Tonga and Samoa, as early as 1200 B.C. Easter Island (Rapa Nui) was one of the last, being reached in A.D. 500. The

Left: *Elaborate face painting and colorful headdresses, as shown by this modern New Guinean, had deep religious and supernatural significance for the indigenous people of New Guinea. Part of the Melanesian group, New Guineans are dark skinned and look different from the other peoples of Oceania.*

Left: *Polynesian women and girls decorate themselves with flowers, which are often strung together and worn like a necklace called a lei.*

long sea journeys and colonizations were well planned: The Polynesians carried with them in canoes all the plants, such as breadfruit, and animals, such as pigs, needed to continue farming and raising animals for food.

Their canoes were made from planks stitched together by *sennit*, a glue from

Below: *Polynesian canoes had extended side arms, called outriggers, for better balance.*

breadfruit trees. Single canoes, which could carry up to 100 people, reached as long as 108 feet (33 m). Double canoes, which could carry as many as 400 people, were as long as 150 feet (46 m), and could travel up to 3,000 miles (4,828 km) in 20 to 30 days.

Polynesian sailors navigated their way across the vast ocean using the stars and planets of the night sky and by following birds during the day. Over time the Polynesian sailors also found that the ocean currents were useful for navigation.

The idea of the creation coming from the Sky Father and Earth Mother began in central Polynesia about 1,000 years ago. Historians know the myth journeyed from island to island with the migrating Polynesians because it is still told on different islands across Oceania, although the sky and earth have different names. In eastern Polynesia, for example, Rangi is known as Atea, which means "great expanse of sky."

The Maker of All Things

This Tahitian creation myth features the god Tangaroa. Both the story and the deity are found in civilizations throughout Polynesia, although with slight variations.

IN THE BEGINNING there existed only Tangaroa, the creator of all things. He lived alone in a giant shell, which revolved slowly in the lonely darkness of space.

One day Tangaroa cracked open his shell, stood up, and yelled "Is anyone out there?" There was no reply from the darkness so Tangaroa called out again. Still there was no answer. All he heard was the rippling echo of his own booming voice, so he sat back down in his shell and sighed.

Time passed and Tangaroa grew increasingly tired of being alone. Finally, he turned his shell into many different shaped rocks and tons of sand, hoping that the new rocks and sand would talk to him. He called out to his creations but again he heard only the echo of his own voice.

Tangaroa then decided to use parts of himself to create the world. First, he took his backbone and made it into a mountain range with his ribs for the mountain ridges. He turned his insides into big, fluffy clouds, and his flesh became the fatness of the earth. He used his arms and legs to create the earth's great strength.

Then Tangaroa made the water that covered the earth and used his fingernails and toenails to create the scales and shells of all the creatures that he put in the water. From his guts Tangaroa formed lobsters, shrimps, and eels to live in the ocean too. And he used his feathers to make the trees, plants, and shrubs that are still seen in lands around the world.

Next Tangaroa concentrated on the sky and the heavens. He turned his blood hot and forced it to float away from him to make the redness of the skies. (Everything that is red came from Tangaroa's blood, including the red in rainbows.) The head of the great creator remained sacred to him and because he was a mighty god, even once he had created everything, his body remained. Next Tangaroa made the other gods to help him rule over the earth and all its creatures.

Because he himself had emerged from a shell, Tangaroa had given almost everything a shell. The sky is actually a shell, and the gods placed the sun, moon, and stars within it. The ground is actually a shell with stones and water in it. And women are actually shells because babies grow inside them. But the powerful Tangaroa created so many different kinds of shells that no one can ever count or name them all.

Above: *According to the Tahitian myth, Tangaroa, the maker of all things, emerged from a giant shell, created the earth and everything on it, and then gave many of his creations their very own shells.*

Comparing Cultures

Although there were many cultural similarities among the various Polynesian civilizations, there were also differences, usually brought on by differences in environment.

Left: *This late 19th-century illustration shows Maori chiefs wearing traditional ceremonial robes.*

The Tahitian myth of Tangaroa and his shell (see page 18) is repeated in different versions across Polynesia. It is also found in other parts of the world, as far away as Greece and Egypt. One of the most popular heroes, the trickster Maui, is associated not just with Hawaii but also with many of the Polynesian islands, where he was known as Maui-tikitiki-a-Taranga. The spread of this and other myths have helped historians trace the ancient migration of Polynesian colonizers across Oceania (see page 16). Other clues to the process of colonization come from important words, such as the names of plants, which are often very similar even on islands that have had little contact for hundreds of years. Basic tools such as fishhooks and adzes also show a common design in widely separated cultures.

of their myths show that they had a great regard for their past.

Most Polynesians lived in villages or smaller hamlets based on traditional kinship groups. Their societies were hierarchical, meaning that there were sharp differences between chiefs and priests on one hand and commoners on the other. Men's and women's jobs were also divided. Men were responsible for planting, harvesting, fishing, cooking, and building houses and canoes. Women tended fields and animals, especially pigs, gathered food and fuel, prepared food for cooking, and made clothes and household items.

All Polynesians depended on the sea. The sea provided not just fish but also sea mammals like whales, mollusks and crustaceans, and edible seaweed. Women and children collected shellfish along the coasts to use for food but also to make jewelry and tools. On some islands strings of seashells even served as a kind of ceremonial money.

Above: *Modern Melanesian women gather banana leaves in the same way their ancestors would have done.*

A CONSERVATIVE CULTURE

Similarities between the cultures in the highly varied environments of Polynesia, where islands vary from rocky volcanic outcrops to raised coral atolls, suggest that the early settlers of the region were very conservative. Many

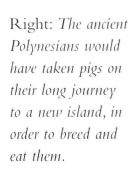

Right: *The ancient Polynesians would have taken pigs on their long journey to a new island, in order to breed and eat them.*

Maui Steals Fire

The trickster Maui is a very popular Polynesian mythological character, capable of both aiding and hindering humans. This Hawaiian myth shows Maui at his naughtiest.

ONCE WHEN MAUI the trickster was bored, he decided to extinguish all the fires in the world. He wanted to see what would happen if there was no fire. This was a long time ago during an age when fire could only be given to the people by Maui's grandmother Mahuika, the goddess of fire.

During the night, while everyone slept, Maui doused all the fires. The next morning, as people woke up and started to prepare breakfast they discovered their fires had gone out. Nobody could cook breakfast or heat water in any of the villages, and they anxiously gathered to discuss what to do.

When Maui's mother realized what had happened, she called her servants and told them to go to Mahuika and ask for some fire. But they were too scared of the goddess and refused to go. Maui said he wanted to go, and so his mother explained how to find the fire goddess's house. She warned her son not to play any tricks on Mahuika but to be polite and respectful to her.

Maui left his village. After a long journey he finally reached the house of the fire goddess. It took him some time to pluck up the courage to speak to her. When he eventually asked her to restore fire to all the villages, Mahuika first wanted to know who he was and where he had come from. "Do you come from where the wind that blows on me comes?" she asked. Maui replied that he did. "You are my grandchild then," replied Mahuika, who then offered him fire. She did so by pulling out one of her fingernails and giving it to him. As she pulled the nail, fire flowed from her finger. Maui took the nail and left.

He had not gone very far before the fire had gone out. So he returned to the goddess. She gave him another nail and off he went again. But Maui soon returned, explaining that the second fire had also gone out. Mahuika removed a third nail, and exactly the same thing happened. Maui carried on the trick until Mahuika had given him all her fingernails and most of her toenails. Finally, Mahuika realized that Maui was tricking her — he wanted to see what happened when she had no nails left. She threw her last nail onto the ground and immediately fire spread everywhere. Maui tried to put out the flames but failed. He turned himself into a hawk to soar above the fire, but his feathers were scorched, which is why the hawk's feathers are black.

Maui called on his ancestor Tawhiri-matea to send rain. Great clouds formed and the rain lashed down. The water level rose until only Mahuika's head remained dry. She lost all her special powers in the deluge. When Maui returned to his parents they saw his burns and soon guessed what had happened. They scolded him, but Maui was unrepentant.

Above: *Ancient Hawaiians feared wildfires, which could spread quickly through forests and destroy whole villages. Maui's escapade with Mahuika's finger- and toenails shows just how reckless the trickster could be.*

Polynesian Beliefs, Taboos, and *Mana*

Myths and religious rules played an important part in the life of Oceania, and certain rituals were practiced everyday in order to maintain a well-structured society and to please the gods.

Left: *Dancing is still an important part of Polynesian life and culture.*

Of all the heroes and villains of Polynesian myth, Maui is the most famous. His popularity stretches across the Pacific, from New Zealand to Hawaii. One of the Hawaiian islands was even named after him. Tricksters appear in many mythologies, like Coyote in Native American myths. They were all contradictory beings; they could be helpful or they could be destructive, as in "Maui Steals Fire" (see page 22). They got their name because they loved to play tricks on people and other gods.

But tricksters could also perform great deeds that benefited humankind. Maui was mostly a hero, though he was often a very naughty one. His good deeds included bringing fire from the underworld, slowing down the sun, and even pulling islands out of the ocean — all to help people.

Myths were at the center of Polynesian life, and the mythology was fairly consistent across Oceania, even though the names of deities were often different. For instance, Tangaroa, the powerful sky god, is referred to as Tagaloa on various islands.

In general, the Polynesian gods shared responsibility for different aspects of daily life, such as cultivating crops, controlling the ocean and fishing, the forests, and the outcome of war. The priests, who were charged with communicating with the gods, were responsible both for the spiritual well-being of the group and for maintaining the oral tradition of myth telling. Because of their responsibilities, priests held a special place of power in

Above: *Images of deities, such as Pele, were often carved out of wood.*

the island community, similar to the one held by chiefs, who were at the top of society (see page 33).

HAWAIIAN KUMULIPO

Since there were no written languages, Polynesian myths and legends were passed on through retelling, usually by the priests. This was often done by chanting, as in the Hawaiian creation myth known as "Kumulipo." The chant tells the story of how the world evolved from primordial slime and then divided into male and female before different stages of life formed, beginning with simple sea creatures and ending with humans. Finally, once everything had been created, day dawned and the world as we know it was established. The chant stresses that there is no supreme creator and that the most important thing is fertility and reproduction.

Tapu and *Mana*

Every activity was defined as being either sacred or not allowed. Those that were not allowed were considered *tapu* — from which comes the English word "taboo." The concept of *tapu* was recognized across Polynesia.

Another fundamental concept was that of *mana*, or personal spiritual power.

Left: *Special objects, such as this carved lizard, had* mana.

Polynesians believed that everybody possessed even a little *mana*, although priests and chiefs had much more of it than others. A person's *mana* could be increased through personal achievements, such as bravery in battle.

Maui and the Sun

This Maori myth about Maui gives a positive portrayal of the trickster. The myth also shows that the gods can sometimes try to make things better for humans.

MAUI WAS THE YOUNGEST of five sons, but when he was born his brothers had not known that their mother, Taranga, was pregnant. He was born prematurely and his mother did not expect him to survive. So she wrapped him in a tuft of her hair and threw him into the ocean. But she prayed that he might survive. And he did not drown; instead, seaweed formed around him and soft jellyfish protected him. Eventually an ancestor, Tama of the sky, found him and hung him up on his rafters over a fire until the infant Maui revived.

Maui stayed with Tama until he was a young man. One day he decided that he wanted to go in search of his real parents. He found his mother and his brothers at a dance at the great assembly house. He sat by his brother, and when it was time to go home and their mother counted her sons, Maui said, "I am your child too." At first Taranga refused to believe it, but Maui soon persuaded her by telling her the names of the whole family. She wept with joy when she realized that Maui had survived being thrown into the sea. From that day on, Maui lived with Taranga and his brothers.

Every day he amazed his brothers with his special powers. Once Maui noticed that no sooner were fires lit to make the day's food than it started to go dark, since the days were very short. He thought that everyone's lives would be much easier if the sun stayed longer in the sky. He talked to his brothers and persuaded them to help him with his plan. He took the enchanted jawbone of his grandmother and set off with his brothers. They journeyed all night, hiding themselves from the sun.

After traveling for several nights they reached the edge of the pit out of which the sun emerged each day (in the Hawaiian version of this myth the pit is the top of Haleakala volcano, which dominates the island of Maui). On the sides of the pit they built a long high wall of clay. When each side of the pit had a wall the brothers set up a noose, making sure that it was as strong as possible. Then they waited until Maui gave them the go-ahead.

As dawn broke, the sun started to rise out of the pit. As it gradually ascended, the sun's head was soon in the noose. Maui shouted and he and all his brothers pulled as hard as they could on the ropes. The sun tried to fight its way out of the noose, but the more it fought the harder the brothers tugged on the ropes. Maui leapt onto the sun and hit its head with the enchanted jawbone to slow it down. The mighty blow worked, so that today the sun travels much slower across the sky, and people have longer to enjoy daylight and do all their daily chores.

Above: *By slowing down the sun Maui made the days longer and sunsets, such as this one over the Pacific island of Bora Bora, more lingering and dramatic for all Polynesians.*

Maori Life and Society

The Polynesians who settled in New Zealand are known as Maori. They have a rich culture, full of expert craftwork and carvings. They were also fearsome warriors.

The Maori were grateful to Maui and his brothers for slowing down the sun because it gave them more time each day to accomplish their many daily tasks (see page 26). The earliest settlers of New Zealand, or "Aotearoa" as the Maori called it, who arrived in about A.D. 800, survived by hunting, fishing, and gathering food. Adapting to their new home must not have been easy since New Zealand is larger and cooler than the other islands settled by the Polynesians. This meant that many of the crops the settlers brought with them in the canoes, such as coconut and breadfruit, would not grow.

Daily tasks were organized according to gender. Men prepared agricultural plots and women planted the seeds. Men fished and dived for shellfish, while women and slaves cooked. One of the staple foods, the fern root, required heavy, time-consuming pounding by women before it could be eaten. In addition to the daily hunting and food preparation, early Maori settlers had to make clothes, build housing, and perform their sacred duties.

Left: *Maori tribal meetinghouses, such as this one built in 1842, were often decorated with elaborate carvings of gods and chiefs.*

They lived in communities, known as *iwi*, that varied in size from a few families to more than 500 people. As Maori society grew more advanced and the people learned to cultivate vegetables — such as taro, kumara (sweet potato), yam, gourds, and paper mulberry — and exploit the creatures of the ocean and forest, they had more

Left: *The Maori war dance not only frightened the enemy but also fired up the warriors.*

time to pursue other interests. They became increasingly warlike and built fortified villages to protect their tribe against enemy Maori tribes.

The Maori felt a strong bond with their ancestors and their creator gods and strongly believed that such spirits and deities could aid them in battle. To show their gratitude and devotion to the gods, the Maori performed elaborate dance-and-song routines, many of which survive among the modern-day Maori.

SKILLED WOODCARVERS

With increased leisure time, the Maori men became sophisticated woodcarvers. Despite having no metal tools, they practiced woodcarving using chisels made out of basalt or greenstone (jade). Some of the best examples of their carving skills are the ornate decorations of canoes, particularly war canoes. These craft, up to 80 feet (24 m) long, were intricately carved on the bow and stern. Even more elaborate were the *whare whakairo*, or carved meetinghouses, where each tribe met and in front of which they performed their sacred religious rites and ceremonies.

Below: *Long and finely carved, Maori war canoes could carry many warriors.*

Maui Reels in the Hawaiian Islands

In this myth the trickster Maui, while fishing with his brothers, reels in a group of islands from the bottom of the ocean. The islands became known as Hawaii.

MAUI AND HIS OLDER brothers fished together many times, but Maui always caught more fish than his brothers. His secret was that he used barbs on his hooks. One day his brothers decided to copy Maui and they too started to catch more fish.

Some time later Maui heard that his brothers were planning a fishing trip in their canoe. He asked to go with them, but they refused because they were tired of all his tricks. So he made himself invisible and hid in the canoe anyway. Once they had paddled out to sea and were busy congratulating themselves on having left their younger brother behind, Maui assumed his normal form so they could see him.

"Let's paddle back to shore and dump Maui," said one of the brothers. Not wanting to go back, Maui made the shoreline recede from the boat. The brothers realized that if they did not let him stay he would cause more trouble. Reluctantly they allowed him to remain but only as long as he bailed out whatever water splashed into the canoe. They would not let him fish.

The brothers were about to cast their lines when Maui told them to paddle a bit farther out.

When they reached the spot to which Maui had guided them, the brothers soon caught more fish than their canoe could hold. They had to turn back to shore or risk capsizing.

Maui asked them if he could fish for a while, but his brothers said that there was no more room in the canoe, and anyway he didn't have a hook. "But I have my own hook," replied Maui, and pulled out his grandmother's jawbone.

The brothers refused to give Maui any bait. This time the clever trickster hit the side of his nose until it bled. Then he saturated the line with blood as bait and fixed it to the jawbone hook. As he cast the bloodied fishing line, Maui murmured a special prayer. The jawbone hook sank and soon the line grew taut. The trickster started to reel it in while repeating another special prayer.

It seemed he had caught a huge fish, but when it came to the surface, the brothers could see that the hook was caught in the roof of a house belonging to the grandson of Tangaroa, the great sky god. Pulling harder still, Maui reeled in the eight big islands of Hawaii. The brothers' canoe became grounded at once.

Above: *Pelekunu Valley in Hawaii is typical of the rugged landscape of mountains and valleys Tangaroa created on the islands following the disrespectful behavior of Maui's brothers.*

Maui wanted to give thanks to Tangaroa for providing them with new land, so he told his brothers to wait while he went to perform the proper rites of thanks and to not eat the fish they had caught until he returned. But the brothers grew impatient and hungry, and they started to eat the fish. Tangaroa saw what was happening and grew angry at the lack of respect the brothers showed. To punish them Tangaroa covered the new islands with mountains and valleys, ridges, and deep ravines, making it difficult for people to walk directly from one side of an island to the other.

The Settling of Hawaii

Despite their remote location near the middle of the Pacific Ocean, the Hawaiian islands were settled many centuries before the Europeans arrived in their large schooners.

Left: *A-frame huts such as this one were built especially as a refuge for those Hawaiians who had broken a* tapu *and needed forgiveness.*

Maui reeled Hawaii out of the sea so that the islands could be settled by the Polynesians (see page 30). This took a long time because Hawaii is the world's most isolated archipelago — it lies more than 2,500 miles (4,023 km) from the nearest landmass. Its remoteness meant the islands were some of the last to be settled by the Polynesians. Historians estimate that the first Polynesians arrived in Hawaii around A.D. 400, after sailing from the Marquesas Islands.

In about A.D. 1000, a second migration brought many Tahitians to Hawaii, who over time took control of the islands from the Marquesans. No one knows how many people first inhabited Hawaii, but by the late 18th century there were an estimated 300,000 people living on the islands. (Today about 1.6 million people live in Hawaii.)

For centuries the islands' inhabitants lived simple lives, dominated by fishing, like Maui and his brothers, and existing in harmony with the spirits of nature. The Hawaiians, like other Polynesians, did not only master the techniques of fishing, ship-building, and navigation. They also developed the organization of their society to such a degree that they could cope with problems that arose within it, such as taking in survivors of boat wrecks and caring for families that had been split due to war.

ISLAND DIVISION

Hawaiian society originally had two tiers. The Tahitians controlled the Marquesans. The people were also separated in groups, each with its own chief. The territory of each group was well defined, spreading like a pie slice from the inland mountains to

Below: *A cluster of tall wooden sculptures of Hawaiian gods.*

the sea. This was done so that each group could farm and have access to a variety of foods from the land, including coconuts, bananas, yam, and sweet potatoes, and foods from the sea, such as fish and crabs.

Hawaiians lived in wooden-framed houses with thatched roofs. Their tools were made out of stone, wood, shell, teeth, and bone. They cooked their food in pits heated by hot stones. For entertainment they enjoyed swimming, surfboarding, and wrestling; played different musical instruments, such as the nose flute; and sang songs, many of which were based on the exploits of Maui and the four main gods, Kau, Kanaloa, Ku, and Lono.

Paao and the Hawaiian Dynasty

In the 12th century the simple lives of the Marquesans and Tahitians who lived in Hawaii changed when a powerful Tahitian "kahuna" (priest), called Paao, arrived on the Big Island. He thought the Hawaiians were lazy and not very devout worshipers. Paao built temples and introduced human sacrifices to the gods, which were carried out in the temples. He also introduced the system of *kapu* (see *tapu*, page 25). The

new rules meant that common people could not associate with the ruling class, including chiefs and kahunas, and women were not allowed to eat coconuts, bananas, pork, or certain types of fish.

Paao also decided that the Hawaiian rulers were not competent, so he brought a principal chief from Tahiti to set up a new royal line. The new ruler was called Pili, and Paao became the high priest of the new ruling house.

Pele

The Hawaiian goddess of volcanoes, Pele, is jealous, distrustful, and vengeful. She can spew molten lava over large areas. She lives in Kilauea on the Big Island.

WHEN THE GODDESS Pele left Tahiti and traveled east she was accompanied by a large entourage that included the gods Ku and Lono and many lesser gods. Pele journeyed from island to island looking for a place to settle, but every time she dug a living hole in the ground the sea poured in and drove her out. Eventually, she burrowed into the Kilauea volcano, on the Big Island of Hawaii. When she did not hit water she decided to settle there.

One night while Pele was in a trance, she left her body and followed the sound of a nose flute being played by a musician on a neighboring island. When she got there she took the form of a beautiful woman. The island's chief, Lohiau, instantly fell in love with her. After spending three days with him, Pele said she had to leave but would send for him.

Back home, Pele sent her sister, Hi'iaka, to fetch Lohiau and gave her magic so she could fulfill her duty. Hi'iaka had to use her powers many times on the journey to overcome a series of obstacles. One such trial was defeating the mo'o monsters, who looked like giant lizards. They tried to stop Hi'iaka by making fog and lashing rain, but she ensnared the mo'o monsters in a fast-growing vine.

Hi'iaka's journey took many years. When she finally reached Lohiau, Hi'iaka discovered that the chief had died of longing for the beautiful woman who had abandoned him. Using her powers once again, Hi'iaka captured his spirit and restored it to his body. Then the two of them set off to meet Pele.

Meanwhile, Pele had grown increasingly jealous and suspicious of her sister for taking so long. In her anger, Pele belched up lava streams, destroying everything around her. Pele took on a new form, this time of a prophetess called Pele-ula. In this form she made Hi'iaka play a courtship game for the hand of Lohiau. A wooden stake was placed in front of Lohiau. The point of the game was to hit it with a spinning gourd. Hi'iaka won the game. By now Lohiau was deeply in love with her, but Hi'iaka was a loyal sister and refused to betray Pele.

Hi'iaka finally delivered Lohiau to Pele's pit, but when she saw how everything had been blackened and destroyed, Hi'iaka was so overcome with grief that she embraced Lohiau. Pele grew furious at this and encircled the lovers with flames. The fire consumed Lohiau but Hi'iaka was protected by her own magical powers. Once the flames had died down, Hi'iaka restored Lohiau to his body again and they fled together. Ever since, Pele has been alone. She shows her anger by spewing forth lava and molten debris whenever she thinks about how she believes her sister deceived her.

Above: *Kilauea, the world's most active volcano and the mythological home of the goddess Pele, hurls fiery rocks into the air and sends molten lava flowing over the Hawaiian countryside.*

A Volcanic Land

The Hawaiian islands are made up of a string of volcanic mountains that rose from the bottom of the Pacific. In addition to the eight main islands, there are over 100 others.

Left: *In an ancient Hawaiian ritual a woman places an offering at the Hulu volcano.*

For Hawaiians, past and present, Pele has always been the goddess of volcanoes. Because the Hawaiian islands are volcanic, and many volcanoes on and near the islands are active, this makes Pele an important deity.

According to Hawaiian mythology, Pele lives on the Big Island (see page 34). Her home is the world's most active volcano, Kilauea — more precisely, Halemaumau, the crater rim where she engulfed Hi'iaka and Lohiau in flames. During certain ceremonies the hula — a special dance — is performed in Pele's honor, but people also leave her offerings of coins, flowers, and other gifts at any time of year.

Close to Kilauea's rim grows an ohelo bush with bright red berries. The berries, which are very sour, are said to be Hi'iaka, and before eating them some should be offered to Pele to appease her. Local people also believe that taking away any of the loose volcanic stones from the mountain is like stealing from Pele herself and will

result in prolonged misfortune for the thief. The rule applies to tourists as well as native Hawaiians.

VOLCANIC HOT SPOTS

Kilauea and all the other Hawaiian volcanoes are shield volcanoes. This means they were formed by gentle eruptions that built up layer upon layer of rock over time. As the mountains of lava increased in size, cracks — known as fault or rift zones — appeared in their sides, allowing lava to pour from the sides as well as from the crater.

Kilauea has been active since 1983. Its current series of eruptions is the longest in recent history. The volcano spews out molten lava continuously. During the day steam can be seen pouring from the vents, and at night the mountainsides and summit glow with the red lava.

Kilauea is the most visible and dramatic example of Hawaii's unique geology. The islands are the exposed tips of huge mountains, formed by a crack in the earth's mantle 25 million years ago. Since then, the mantle has continued to spew out molten lava. This

Above: Small, active volcanoes off the Hawaiian coast form new land-masses, just as they have done for millions of years.

Below: Hula dancers perform a special ritual to appease the gods.

"hot spot" is fixed, but the ocean floor lies on the Pacific plate of the earth's crust, which is moving northwest by approximately 3 inches (7.6 cm) a year. When weak spots in the earth's crust pass over the hot spot, molten lava is forced out, creating new volcanoes under the ocean's surface. These new volcanoes will eventually leave behind the hot spot. The farther a new volcano moves from the hot spot, the less active it becomes.

Eventually, some underwater volcanoes emerge above the sea as islands. The Big Island is the most recent to emerge of the Hawaiian chain, and today Kilauea is directly over a hot spot. Southeast of the Big Island, less than 30 miles (48 km) away, a new island is forming and has already built up 15,000 feet (4,572 m) on the ocean floor. In contrast, the islands northwest of the Big Island have been eroded away over millions of years and will eventually disappear.

The Many Battles of the War God Tu

As in many cultures around the world, war was an unavoidable part of Polynesian life. This myth shows the war god Tu's (called Ku in Hawaii) insatiable appetite for conflict.

TU WAS ONE OF THE SONS of Earth Mother and Sky Father who dwelled among the upperworlds (see page 14). He was embroiled in an argument between his brothers, Tane and Tangaroa. Another brother, Tawhiri, father of storms and wind, grew so upset with his brothers' behavior that he turned on them. During the battle between the brothers both Tane and Tangaroa fled, leaving Tu to fight Tawhiri on his own. Although Tu defeated Tawhiri he was angry with his other brothers for having deserted him and decided to take revenge.

Tu made snares to trap Tane's special birds, who lived in his forests. Then he made nets from flax plants so that he could capture the children of Tangaroa. Not satisfied with just hurting Tane and Tangaroa, Tu turned on his other brothers. First he pulled up by the hair — which was actually leaves — the children of his brothers Haumia and Rongo and left them to dry in the sun. He then ate the children.

Despite Tu's victories over his brothers, they continued to wage war. In order to control them, Tu, who was now god of war, learned many different incantations. He chanted spells for plentiful food, for good wind, and to stop his brothers from reigning supreme. He also chanted special words to Earth Mother so that she would produce enough food for everyone, which is how Tu also came to be known as the god of creation.

Tu asked his brother Rongo, who was the father of cultivated food, to help him eject their brothers from the upperworlds. Even though Tu had eaten Rongo's children, he agreed to help.

With Rongo at his side, Tu swept through the different upperworlds, facing no real resistance until the battle of Puke-nui-o-hotu. He and his forces won that fierce battle and then a second victory at Puke-nui-papa. As Tu won further victories, Rongo continually advised him to slay his enemies, but Tu was not particularly interested in killing everyone; it was enough for him just to win the battles and humiliate his brothers.

When they reached the eighth upperworld, the troops of the gods who had been defeated rallied together, and Tu was defeated for the first time at the final battle of Te Uru-rangi. He fell to Kai-hewa, which lies far beneath the earth's surface. He still lives there and continues to incite humans to perform evil acts.

Left: *Red feathers and sharp teeth make this ancient model of the war god appear very fearsome. Captain James Cook collected this model on one of his voyages.*

War and the Polynesians

For many Polynesians, military skirmishes and raids were a common occurrence. Often such conflicts ended in limited damage, but sometimes prisoners were taken and even eaten.

Left: *Traveling in canoes was the only way for Maori warriors to reach other islands for a battle or raid.*

Tu's aggressive, belligerent relationship with his brothers (see page 38) echoed a dominant aspect of Polynesian life — war. From New Zealand to Easter Island, Polynesians fought each other, often for territorial gains.

Throughout their history, Polynesian peoples experienced tension and pressure due to overcrowding on their islands. For example, as population density increased on the islands of New Zealand, the Maori gradually transformed from a peaceful hunter-gatherer people to a fearsome warring nation. They moved from open settlements to heavily fortified villages built on hilltops.

War not only allowed the different Maori tribes to acquire new land and slaves, but it was one of the best ways of promoting *mana*. *Mana* is the spiritual quality of a person, animal, or thing and includes the authority given to chiefs and priests (see page 25).

Mana could be increased or gained by ordinary tribal members through heroic deeds in battle, so the Maori developed into a highly sophisticated warrior society.

War had its own type of worship, sacrifices, rituals, dances, and art forms. One of the most important war items was the war canoe, which was a source of great *mana* for a tribe.

War canoes were built of kauri or totara wood and could be up to 80 feet (24 m) long. Each end of the canoe was elaborately carved by a specially chosen craftsman who had sacred powers. Human figures were the main detail of the carvings, but the carver could not reproduce humans exactly because people are a divine creation and to replicate them was an insult to the gods.

For some tribes, plundering raids rather than full battles could usually settle any dispute between neighbors.

Above: *This jade pendant is believed to possess* mana, *the spiritual quality that could be increased by heroic deeds in battle.*

But tribes who were raided often launched a reprisal raid. This meant that some tribes were in a constant state of warfare (like Tu and his brothers).

CANNIBALISM IN OCEANIA

For all tribes, losing a war could have fearful results. Many cultures, such as the Fijians and the Australian Aborigines, practiced some form of cannibalism. Evidence of cannibalism has been found in many parts of the ancient world. Among Polynesian tribes, including the Maori, defeated warriors either became slaves or were eaten. Eating the enemy was the worst insult one tribe could inflict on another. The Maori ate their enemies because they believed that an enemy's life force would then be passed on to them.

Left: *This mid-19th-century illustration shows Maori warriors cooking and consuming the remains of their defeated enemies. Archaeologists have discovered that similar acts of cannibalism were practiced in many parts of the ancient world and were in no way unique to the Maori.*

The Story of the Wooden *Moai*

On Easter Island, or Rapa Nui, the Polynesians carved wooden figures known as moai kavakava (male) and moai paepae (female). The figures likely had religious importance.

LONG AGO ON THE island of Rapa Nui, after the rule of Hotu Matua, lived Tu-Uko-Ihu, who was the first chief and priest to carve images on the island.

One day Tu-Uko-Ihu decided to visit a site at Hanga known as the House of Cockroaches. He left in the early morning and, in order to reach Hanga, had to climb to Punapau Mountain. There, in front of the red cliff, he saw two spirits who were fast asleep. Unlike humans, the spirits, called Hitirau and Nuku-the-Shark, were not covered by flesh, so the chief could see all their ribs. He hurried past, pretending that he had not seen them. He knew that if the spirits had suspected he had seen them, they would have killed him.

Tu-Uko-Ihu continued his journey but another spirit, Ha-uriuri, saw him and was convinced that he had seen the other spirits. Ha-uriuri woke up Hitirau and Nuku-the-Shark, telling them that they had been seen by a human. As the spirits looked up all they saw was the chief's back as he climbed the mountain.

Immediately the two spirits ran in front of Tu-Uko-Ihu and demanded to know exactly what he had seen. "I saw nothing," replied the chief. The spirits continued to question him as he carried on his journey. Eventually they disappeared and left Tu-Uko-Ihu alone, but they remained suspicious.

When Tu-Uko-Ihu arrived at Hanga the two spirits made themselves invisible and floated around the house where he was staying, waiting for him to tell the other humans what he had seen. But the chief remained silent. When he went to the House of Cockroaches people were busy taking stones out of earth-ovens and throwing out the end pieces of burning wood.

Tu-Uko-Ihu picked up some of the burning wood and with a sharp piece of obsidian carved the wood into *moai kavakava*. The carvings resembled Hitirau and Nuku-the-Shark, with their ribs showing. Having finished carving, Tu-Uko-Ihu fell asleep and dreamed of two women. Their names were Pa-apa ahiro and Pa-apa akirangi. Tu-Uko-Ihu carved them exactly as they appeared in his dream and called them *moai paepae*.

When the people saw the spirit statues Tu-Uko-Ihu had made, they all wanted him to carve more *moai kavakava* and *moai paepae*. In exchange for his carvings people cooked seabirds, fish, and

Above: *This* moai kavakava, *which resembles the carvings made by Tu-Uko-Ihu, was found on Easter Island (Rapa Nui). The* moai kavakava *are the male versions and the* moai paepae *are the female.*

yams in their earth-ovens. Only those people who offered the chief something received one of the carvings.

Several days after Tu-Uko-Ihu had started carving, some villagers went to the chief to ask for images in exchange for the food they had given him. Tu-Uko-Ihu ordered them to wait while he went inside the house and made all the images walk. From that day on, the house was known as the House of Walking Images.

Sculptures of Rapa Nui

The giant stone sculptures that line the edges of Easter Island are an impressive and eerie legacy of the Polynesian inhabitants. But the purpose of the figures remains a mystery.

Left: *Most stone statues on Easter Island faced inland. They were extremely heavy and appear to have been moved by wooden sledges on top of rollers made from logs.*

The *moai kavakava* — or wooden "statues of ribs" — that Tu-Uko-Ihu carved (see page 42) have been found by archaeologists on Easter Island. Each wooden statue is of a human figure with an elongated face with exaggerated features and ribs sticking out of a sunken stomach that suggest starvation. One theory for the unusually emaciated appearance of the wooden statues is that they were carved during a period of food shortage on the island.

Easter Island also has another unique type of statue, far more famous and mysterious than even the *moai kavakava*. These are the massive stone *moai*, which can still be seen on the island.

Lying more than 1,000 miles (1,609 km) from the nearest landmass, Rapa Nui — the island's Polynesian name — is a small volcanic island. It is the most remote of all the Polynesian islands and is also the world's most remote inhabited island. Little is known about the history of the

Polynesians who lived on Rapa Nui, apart from the presence of the large stone *moai* that dominate the island.

MYSTERY OF THE STATUES

Archaeologists know how and where the *moai* were carved — the oldest statues date from the 7th century — but who exactly carved them and what the figures actually represented remain uncertain. Historians believe that gaining a greater understanding of the massive stone statues is the key to unlocking the mystery surrounding the collapse of the Rapa Nui culture in the 18th century.

Today approximately 400 stone statues remain on the island. They vary in height, with the tallest over 30 feet (9 m) and the smallest about 6.5 feet (2 m). No two are the same, although many have similarities. A typical statue has a long, rectangular face with a big nose, thin lips, heavy brows, and elongated earlobes. The body has a protruding stomach and elaborately

carved back that might represent tattooing. On either side of the body hang stiff arms with long, slender hands.

The statues line the island's shore, mostly facing inland. A current theory is that the statues are figures of chiefs and priests, facing inland to watch over their respective kin groups. The statues were carved out of volcanic rock at a quarry on the island. Uncompleted statues have been found in the quarry still in the rock face.

Above: *As shown in this 1875 illustration, French sailors removed several Rapa Nui stone statues to take back to Europe. The removal of the sacred monuments outraged the native islanders.*

Obsessive Carving

Many anthropologists think that the islanders became so obsessed with carving stone statues that they neglected their other duties, such as cultivating food. Lack of food and overpopulation led to fighting. This might explain why many of the statues now lie on the ground, possibly having been pushed over during a period of clan warfare in the 18th century that began the long collapse of Rapa Nui culture. Cutting down most of the island's trees, which were needed for building and as fuel, may also have helped speed the collapse of the island's civilization.

Glossary

Aotearoa The Maori name for New Zealand.

Austronesian A Melanesian language group.

Black-headed Python Grieving widow of **Native Cat**. She created and named many things following the death of her husband.

Blue-tongued Lizard In Aborigine mythology, a friend of **Native Cat** and **Black-headed Python**.

Cook, James (1728–1779) British naval captain and explorer. He visited and charted many islands in the Pacific, including Tahiti, New Zealand, Australia, Easter Island, the Marquesas, Tonga, and finally Hawaii, where he was killed.

Dreamtime An age when humans and the natural world were created. Many Australian Aborigines believe that it continues and is where ancestral spirits live.

Footprints of the Ancestors Aborigines believe that the whole of the Australia is connected by an ancient series of invisible tracks, also called "songlines." Aborigines travel along the songline of their group and sing the songs of their ancestors.

green parrot women Sister deities who were attacked by their brother **Tjinimin**. They later took their revenge on him.

Haumia-tiketike The Maori god of uncultivated food and one of the sons of **Rangi** and **Papa**.

Hi'iaka The sister of **Pele**, she was loyal but eventually driven away by the volcano goddess's jealousy.

Hitirau One of the fleshless spirits on Easter Island who **Tu-Uko-Ihu** saw and based the *moai* on.

hot spot A crack in the earth's mantle formed some 25 million years ago out of which molten lava still flows. Hot spots on the ocean floor create volcanic islands, such as the Big Island of Hawaii.

House of Walking Images The place on Easter Island where **Tu-Uko-Ihu** carved the *moai*.

hula A Hawaiian ritual dance performed in honor of **Pele**.

iwi A Maori community.

kahuna A Polynesian priest.

Kai-hewa The place far inside the earth where the war god **Tu** fell.

kapu Social restrictions imposed by **Paao** that forbade the working class from interacting with the ruling class and prevented women from eating pork and certain other foods.

Kilauea Located on the Big Island of Hawaii, it is the world's most active volcano and home of the goddess **Pele**.

Ku A deity who traveled with the volcano goddess **Pele** from Tahiti.

Kumulipo A Hawaiian chant that tells the story of how the world and its creatures evolved.

Lohiau The island chief with whom **Pele** fell in love.

Lono A Hawaiian deity who traveled with the volcano goddess **Pele** from Tahiti.

Mahuika The goddess of fire; in Hawaiian mythology she was the grandmother of **Maui**.

mana Personal spiritual power, which could be possessed by both living things and objects.

Maui A Polynesian trickster, also called Maui-tikitiki-a-Taranga. He caused mischief but did good too.

moai kavakava The wooden sculptures first made by **Tu-Uko-Ihu** that resemble the male spirits on Easter Island.

moai paepae The wooden sculptures made by **Tu-Uko-Ihu** that resemble the female spirits on Easter Island.

Native Cat In Aboriginal mythology, the husband of **Black-headed Python**. He died and was brought back to life by his friend **Blue-tongued Lizard**.

Nuku-the-Shark One of the fleshless spirits **Tu-Uko-Ihu** saw on Easter Island.

Paao A powerful **kahuna** from Tahiti who established the Hawaiian royal family and introduced human sacrifice to Hawaii.

Papa See **Rangi**.

Pele The Hawaiian goddess of volcanoes. She lives in the world's most active volcano, **Kilauea**.

Pili The first ruler of the Tahitian-born Hawaiian royal family introduced to the islands by **Paao**.

Pilirin the Kestrel In Aboriginal mythology, he gave fire to the

Aborigines by rubbing two sticks together to create sparks.

Rainbow Snake In Aboriginal mythology, the father of **Tjinimin** and the **green parrot women**. After he was wounded by his son, his blood created many things, including water sources in the Outback.

Rangi In Maori mythology, one of the two parent-gods. He was the sky god and loved **Papa**, the earth goddess. The two were separated from their tight embrace by their son, **Tane-mahuta**.

Rongo Brother of **Tu** who helped him battle their brothers for control of the upperworlds.

Rongo-ma-Tane The Maori god of cultivated food and one of the sons of **Rangi** and **Papa**.

Tama An ancestor of **Maui** who rescued the trickster from the sea.

Tane-mahuta The Maori god of forests and everything in them. One of the sons of **Rangi** and **Papa**.

Tangaroa The Maori god of all things living in the sea, he was one of the sons of **Rangi** and **Papa**. In a Tahitian creation myth he emerged from a shell. And in a Hawaiian myth he gave the Hawaiian islands to **Maui** and his brothers, but in anger made them mountainous.

tapu The practice of identifying certain forbidden or sacrilegious acts. It is the source of the English word "taboo."

Tawhiri-matea The Maori god of winds and storms, and one of the sons of **Rangi** and **Papa**. In

Hawaiian mythology he was an ancestor of **Maui** the trickster.

Tjinimin the Bat From Aboriginal mythology, a **Dreamtime** deity who tried to kill his father, **Rainbow Snake**.

Tu Polynesian war god who ended up deep inside the earth in **Kai-hewa**, from where he incites men to perform bad deeds.

Tu-matauenga The Maori god of war and one of the sons of **Rangi** and **Papa**.

Tu-Uko-Ihu The first priest on Easter Island to carve the wooden statues known as *moai*.

whare whakairo A Maori carved meetinghouse in front of which tribes performed rituals.

Further Reading & Viewing

BOOKS

Beaglehole, J. C., et al. *The Journals of Captain James Cook.* New York, NY: Penguin Classics, 2000.

Bell, R. *Visit to Australia.* Westport, CT: Heinemann, 1999.

Hermes, Jules. *The Children of Micronesia.* Minneapolis, MN: Carolrhoda Books, 1994.

McCollum, Sean. *A Ticket to Australia.* Minneapolis, MN: Carolrhoda Books, 1999.

Ngcheong-Lum, Roseline. *Fiji.* Tarrytown, NY: Benchmark Books, 2000.

Nilsen, Robert. *Moon Handbooks: Big Island of Hawaii.* New York, NY: Avalon Travel Publications, 2001.

Sammis, Fran. *Australia and the South Pacific.* Tarrytown, NY: Benchmark Books, 2000.

Sigurdsson, Haraldur, et al. *Encyclopedia of Volcanoes.* San Diego, CA: Academic Press, 1999.

VIDEOS

National Geographic's Australia's Aborigines. National Geographic, 1997.

National Geographic's Hawaii: Strangers in Paradise. National Geographic, 1991.

New Zealand. Questar Inc., 1998.

Nova: Secrets of the Lost Empires II: Easter Island. WGBH Boston, 2000.

WEBSITES

Aborigines: The First Australians. http://www.ozramp.net.au/~senani/aborigin.htm.

Maori Resources Online. http://www.culture.co.nz.

Index